The Long Look Inward

CORY SKILLERN

For Jess, Leyton, Landon, Ledger & Lake

"The longest journey is the journey inward."

— Dag Hammarskjöld

First Edition

ISBN: 979-8-9952150-1-1

Published by Long Road Society Press
Eastvale, California

Printed in the United States of America

TABLE OF CONTENTS

I — THE WORLD AS I SEE IT

Late Night Stroll

The crickets and frogs play their songs,
with the faint roar of a passing plane,
and the domino howling at a cat prowling.
In the distance, a whistle of a train.

A bird takes flight on the cool summer night,
chirping along the way.
The ovation of leaves in the nocturnal breeze
on a moonlit stroll down the lane.

The night symphony puts me at ease;
the stress of the day is washed away.

The Passerby

The controlled chaos
of a metropolitan sidewalk.
What they're wearing,
the subtle seduction
of a sweet perfume,
the exhaust from a rumbling engine,
the stench rising off a trash can—
each one triggers a memory in the rush.
All of it passing in the same breath.
Everyone looking but not seeing,
it seems that those who know you the least
are the ones who judge you the most.

Alone Together

How is it social
when it leaves people feeling alone,
scrolling through strangers
while ignoring the ones at home?

We call it media
as if it carries truth,
as if a feed full of filters
could ever show proof.

It promises connection
but trades it for display
a thousand tiny performances
to get us through the day.

It tells us who to envy,
who to follow, who to be,
yet somehow leaves us emptier
than who we were originally.

We post our brightest moments
to hide the darker ones inside,
hoping someone out there sees us,
hoping someone feels the tide.

But the irony is simple:
the more we try to be seen,
the more invisible we feel
behind the cold screen.

So, tell me,

what's social about isolation?
What's media about pretending?

Maybe it's just a mirror
we keep mistaking for a window,
a place we go to feel connected
and end up feeling hollow.

Fortunate

Laboring in the yard,
with a dozen other things
I wished I was doing,
I paused for a break,
accidentally taking in the moment.
As I sat and basked
in the sunshine's gentle warmth,
I heard fountains murmuring, insects buzzing,
birds jabbing the air with their calls,
distant voices drifting through the afternoon,
a dog barking somewhere out of sight,
the faint hum of traffic on the street,
a plane carving its slow path overhead,
two hummingbirds sparring for nectar.
A light breeze moved through,
and the world kept turning.
And in that stillness,
I realized I was exactly
where I was meant to be—
sole witness to nature's work,
honored just to be there,
fortunate enough to notice.

Eternity

I know one day I'm going to die,
so, what will any of this mean to me?
Some people believe we will fly
to heaven, carried on wings.

Others believe most will go to hell,
cast to the pits of lost desire,
where echoes of the fallen swell,
eternally bound to judgment's fire.

Some folks believe we'll be born anew,
in realms where dreams and hopes reside.
While others think we'll fade from view,
like whispers lost in the open sky.

Some think we'll just turn to dust,
mingle with the earth, disappear.
No dreams, no fire, no heaven's trust,
just stillness in the atmosphere.

II — THE SHAPE OF ME

Inheritance

There's no manual for this work,
no right way to raise a family —
just showing up
and hoping you're enough.

My parents never complained.
They hid their own struggles,
set their pain aside.
Waking before the sun,
long shifts to keep us fed,
making sure we were ready
for each day.

They held us accountable,
taught us manners and morals,
cooked the meals,
did the repetitive things
that matter more than anyone admits.

They loved without conditions,
stood on the sidelines of practices and games,
unwavering, supportive, present.

This is my inheritance —
not money, not things,
but the way they live.
And I want to pass it on.

When the World Felt Bigger

I miss the days before cell phones.
Don't get me wrong—
I'm guilty of keeping mine close,
checking it more than I should,
letting it tug at my attention
like a small, persistent child.

But I don't like the addiction,
or the way being chronically reachable
has rewired us.
Everyone always knows where you are,
and if they don't,
panic blossoms in the silence—
a fear that never existed before.

There was an innocence then.
The world felt bigger,
not because it was,
but because we were analog.

We played outside with our friends—
not the "friends" in our phones
or online—
but the ones who lived down the street,
the ones who could catch our pass,
the ones who knew our laugh.

We didn't need a ride.
We just rode our bikes over
to see if they could play.

We were expected home by a certain time,
and we knew the hour
by the watch on our wrist
or the streetlights flickering on
as the sun slipped away.

We had to look for a flashlight—
we didn't carry one in our pockets.
We didn't have a map of everyone's life
unfolding in real time.
We didn't have to keep up with anyone—
their vacations,
their remodels,
their carefully selected happiness.
We only saw the world in front of us,
and that was enough.

Now the whole world fits in our hand,
and somehow feels smaller for it.
We traded patience for immediacy,
privacy for visibility,
being here for being seen.

And I can't help wondering
if the price we pay now
is far greater
than the convenience we gained.

The Older I Get

The older I get, the more I see
I'm not as intelligent as I once believed.
The world isn't black and white—
just blurred lines and shifting greys.

I catch myself becoming a hypocrite,
acting like the people I once despised.
I regret things I've said,
now that I understand my own ignorance—
yet, I keep saying things
I'll later wish I hadn't.

The fantasy world of my youth has faded.
My parents are human after all,
not flawless and larger-than-life as I once
imagined.
Nothing is perfect
the way I once believed.

Now it's my turn
to build a cushioned box for my children,
though I've never known how to build.
My turn to shape their world as "perfect,"
knowing one day
I'll disappoint them too.

Drawer Poems

There are poems I never finished,
words crossed out, scribbled and scratched,
and poems I completed
but couldn't let out into the world—
sentenced to life in the drawer.

Some were too pointed,
some too private,
some said more than I meant to say.

A few were written in the dark
and stayed there—
folded once, then again,
slipped into a drawer
with the things I keep
but don't display.

They're not failures.
They're not secrets.
They're just pieces of me
that didn't want an audience.

Sometimes I open the drawer
and read a line or two.
Sometimes I check
that they're still there.

Most days I forget
what's even on those pages.

But every so often,

a poem I never meant to share
teaches me something
about the one I'm writing now.

And I realize
those hidden pages—
the ones no one will ever see—
are holding up the rest of the work
from underneath.

They don't need a title.
They don't need a reader.
They only need a place to rest.

So, I keep them
where they belong—
in the drawer,
in the dark,
still doing their job
serving their time
long after I've moved on.

The Night Sky

When I was younger,
I thought every person I met
would be part of my life—
a whole sky of stars
I expected to guide me forever.
Some burned out quietly.
Some were never stars at all,
just brief flashes
I mistook for something lasting.
The satellites drifted—
circling close for a while,
then slipping out of range,
their signal fading
until only distance remained.
But when they returned,
they returned completely,
as if no time had passed,
as if nothing had shifted
between us.
And some
were only meant to pass through—
bright for a moment,
gone the next,
leaving fragments behind,
small pieces of clarity
from when they moved
through my life.
I used to think the distance
was a failure—
as if I'd done something wrong,
as if trying harder

might have kept them in orbit.
But not every connection
is meant to circle back.
Not everything that mattered
was meant to stay.
With age, the sky grew smaller.
Not from loss,
but from clarity—
I learned which stars are real,
which ones remain
to light the way
without demanding anything
in return.
Now I keep a small constellation—
Just enough to walk my path,
just enough to maintain
without losing my way.

The Last One Left

Last spring, in my infancy,
Indistinguishable from the next,
The others with surprising apathy,
While I was more complex.

I had an innate ambition.
They would trust the breeze;
I'd long for something more
than the other leaves.

I was one of many
but was determined to be unique.
Something in me was uncanny —
that's what made me distinct.

Seasons altered drastically.
Summer turned to Fall;
colors changed vividly,
affecting one and all.

The weather was very harsh.
The wind proved a formidable foe.
Some just could not hang on
when it started to blow.

My friends began to wither,
slowly falling one by one.
And as the cold became bitter,
eventually they were all gone.

I'm all alone now
In this brisk winter air.
The sun gave way to heavy clouds;
The branches are bleak and bare.

The first snow flake has fallen
on this morn damp and drear.
Looming shadows sprawling—
it seems the end is near.

I take great pride knowing,
through the thick of it,
that I kept going
when all of the others quit.

This is my final request:
as I bid farewell to my gracious host,
remember, I was different from the rest,
and that's what matters most.

Self

Long before "I" was,
when something sparked itself into being.
A small warmth in the dark.
No pride. Not pried.
Just existence.
That first flame.
Then came the stacking—
impressions forming a story,
experiences and lessons and voices and losses
arranging themselves like bricks in a Jenga tower
I learned to call "me".
Sometimes I think it started
on that old hallway carpet,
the one I walked half awake,
worn thin under my feet,
trying to understand the house
and the person forming inside it.
Desire followed, sudden as weather.
A pull toward what I didn't have
and couldn't yet name.
I wanted love,
and then I wanted more.
I wanted safety,
and then I wanted freedom.
The wanting gave me direction,
gave me momentum.
The wanting taught me hunger.
Pain branded me
before I understood it.
The "self" hardened,
built walls,

built stories to explain the walls.
Suffering became a tutor—
rigid, uninvited—
showing me where "I" end
and where "I" break.
Eventually, I turned inward
and saw the grinding gears:
the defenses,
the narratives,
the lies I told myself
to stay intact.
It wasn't flattering.
But honesty, I learned,
is a kind of mercy.
So, I loosened my grip.
Just enough to breathe.
Edges frayed,
stories thinned.
I realized not everything
needed to become mine.
Some things could pass through
without touching my soul.
And still, I remain.
A self that remembers,
that wants,
that suffers,
that keeps trying to understand
Ever evolving,
Unfinished.

The Salmon

I was made for the rough water—
the kind that pushes back,
the kind that asks
how badly I want to keep going.
Upstream is the only direction
my body seems to understand.
Not because I'm stubborn—
well, I am—
but because something in me
was shaped by resistance.
Most creatures let the river
decide their direction.
I move through the places
that try to turn me around.
There are easier paths,
I've seen them—
wide, smooth,
the others moving together.
But my life has been
cold water,
sharp stones,
getting to where I'm meant to be.
And still I swim,
not to prove anything,
not to win anything,
but because moving against the current
has always felt right to me,
never once a reason to stop.

Understanding

When I was a kid,
my parents were immortal.
They knew everything.
They stood larger than life,
and the world felt safe
because they were there.
I never saw the work behind it—
the teaching, the molding,
the raising of a boy
into someone who might one day
be good.
Then the teenage years came,
and I thought I knew better.
My world felt bigger than theirs,
so, what could they possibly tell me?
Still, they stayed—
steady, supportive,
giving me space to learn myself.
I could've asked them anything,
but I didn't.
Maybe I feared the answer,
or the look on their face,
or the truth about why I was asking.
Adulthood didn't change that.
The distance just grew quieter.
But when we had kids of our own,
something shifted.
I saw my parents clearly—
not as giants,
but as humans
who carried more than I ever noticed,

who loved me in ways
I never thanked them for.
It's unfortunate
how late understanding arrives,
how gratitude waits
for the right moment.
Now, I just hope
my kids will one day
see me with the same grace
I finally see in my parents—
not perfect,
just trying,
just here,
just theirs.

III — THE LONG LOOK INWARD

The Blue Dragonfly

I sat on the edge, legs hanging over the water,
brushing away the gnats that hovered and
hummed.
A small fish surfaced, curious,
then slipped back into the dark without a sound.

The clouds were gathering, thick and grey,
the air cooling the way it does before a storm.
Then a blue dragonfly settled on my hand—
light as breath, steady, as if he knew me.

I didn't understand why he chose me,
or why he left so quickly.
But the warmth he brought stayed with me,
long after his wings lifted him away.

And the moment he was gone,
the first drop of rain found me.

The After

In the first days, everyone shows up—
neighbors, cousins you haven't seen in years,
people who don't know what to say
but say it anyway.

Cards pile up.
Meals arrive.
Your phone won't stop buzzing.

Then it fades.

Visits become texts.

Then nothing.

Comfort in distance.

You're left with your thoughts,
your tears,
and a coffee table covered in gift cards
and well wishes.

Panic

Confined within the prison of my mind,
an endless weight of unrest.
I search for peace I cannot find,
gasping, reaching for the next breath—

Distractions

Please take me somewhere else,
away from the threatening silence
where panic dwells.

Pull me from these intrusive thoughts,
free me from this nightly despair,
loosen the mental knots
that ride in on the night air.

Let me breathe deeper in my soul,
slow the fast-paced thumping of my heart,
begin to take back control
as the storm inside me parts.

Night Always Comes

When the noise of the kids quiets down,
and my wife falls fast asleep,
I click the remote and set it down—
into the night, my worries creep.

Most nights I toss and turn;
I can't get out of my own head.
Uncomfortable, restless legs,
anxiety filling me with dread.

I worry more these days—
about time, and how it slips.
How fragile our lives feel,
how fast the years eclipse.

I'm noticing it now
more sharply than before:
people who looked young just years ago
look older now—as do I, I'm sure.

Mortality scares me—
one less day crossed off my life.
In the darkness, these thoughts haunt me,
piercing the silence like a knife.

But dawn will wake, the night will sleep,
and with the light, the shadows retreat.
By day the fears all fade away—
until night returns, and dread replays.

The Long Storm

I watched the rain clouds come in that day.
The sky darkened, as if someone pulled a blanket
over the sun
and told it to sleep.
No one else seemed to notice—
not the thunder clapping with anger,
not the sharp electricity striking the ground.

Just me.

The storm came in short bursts at first,
then stretched into weeks,
then months,
then years.
I wondered if I should just stay out in it,
let the water rise over my head,
stop looking for reprieve.

Then I noticed others walking through the same
downpour,
each of them holding umbrellas.
I thought I was alone
until they showed me, I wasn't.

Over time, the clouds thinned.
Occasionally, a small ray would puncture through,
giving glimpses of hope.

And one day the sun pulled the sky open
and showed its face again.
It revealed what the darkness had been hiding:

the beauty that had been there all along,
too engulfed by the storm for me to see.

House

Dented and punctured from the normal wear,
so many lives have moved through here.
Pinned up and banged on, I do not care—
I have witnessed all the laughs and tears.

Spills, leaks, and breaks,
transformations subtle or extreme,
the kind a lived-in lifetime makes,
and every change these walls have seen.

I stand through it all,
weathered but steady,
a shelter shaped by every fall,
and always holding myself ready.

Comfort in Distance

Why do I like that faint smell of devastation?
It reaches me so calmly.
The familiar amber glow in the sky—
maybe it's because I'm far enough away
that a raging forest fire
reaches me like a bonfire—
warm, familiar,
almost inviting—
even as it tears something else apart.

The Lizard

I went in the backyard today
just to throw something in the trash bin.
Almost automatic.
Nothing important.
I saw something in the pathway.
At first, I thought it was a leaf.
As I got closer, I realized it was a lizard.
But when I neared, it didn't scurry away.
I nudged it gently with my foot.
It only blinked… seemed like such a heavy task.
It must've been sick.
Dying.
A small life,
Alone in the open,
Waiting for whatever comes next.

Under the Surface

I dropped a line in the lake,
as I was obliged to do.
The surface held still, mirrored,
only a small ripple off my bobber.

But under that calm,
the lake was busy with its own unrest,
currents shifting, pressures changing,
a whole world I couldn't see.

Nothing tugged the line,
yet I felt the truth of it:
how calm things can look
when so much is happening
underneath.

It Rattles the Windows

It still shows up,
Not as frequent but
It rattles the windows
just to remind me it's there.
It comes and goes
like the ocean's tide—
branches knocking together,
leaves and dust spinning in the air.
I know it will still move through me.
Sometimes a slight push,
sometimes a hard shove.
But I brace for it now.
I know it's temporary.
I know it passes.
And I don't lose myself in it
the way I used to.

The Long Look Inward

I wander through the night,
in shadows cast by choices made.
Pacing in the moonlight,
a heart weighed down by what remains.

Each step I take on paths once bright,
now fading into grey.
The whispers of the past unite
and follow me each day.

The dreams I chased, the chances lost—
they linger in my mind.
Regret, a ghost of heavy cost,
in memory I find.

The days I let slip through my hands
like sand along the shore
return in waves as time expands,
a truth I can't ignore.

Yet in this maze of sorrow's grasp
a flicker breaks the dark—
a hope that I might slip the past
and light may find my heart.

For though the past may hold me tight,
its grip can let me go.
And in the dawn of morning light,
new paths and dreams can grow.

IV — THE CENTER OF GRAVITY

Microcosmic

Nebulas glowing in the dark,
galaxies drifting in slow circles,
the universe doing what it's always done
moving, expanding,
more than we'll ever understand.

So many complexities,
so many moving parts,
everything shifting, colliding.
Billions of stars falling into place
far beyond our control.

And somehow,
in all that chaos,
everything aligned perfectly
for our worlds to collide.

All the forces at play,
all the quiet motions
we never saw coming—
they brought me to you.

Two small lives
in a universe too big to measure,
yet somehow, we fit,
like two puzzle pieces.

A whole world
inside the space between us.
A microcosm
made of you and me.

That Time…

We met young
and somehow stayed long enough
to build a life out of nothing—
three kids, too many cats,
dogs I swore I didn't want,
a house near a school
we once couldn't afford.

Sometimes I think about
how fragile it all was,
how easily we could've missed each other.

If I'd met you on a bad day,
a tired day,
a don't-touch-me, don't-talk-to-me day—
one of those days
where the world feels too loud
and everything hurts—

maybe none of this
would've happened.

And God,
what a loss
that would've been.

The Way She Sleeps

She can sleep anywhere,
on the couch or on a plane.
But it's not about where she sleeps.
It's the way she sleeps—
comfortable, warm, deeply.
Each time she exhales,
she lets the day fall off her,
telling it to wait again for tomorrow,
because right now, it's her time,
and something in me settles —
envious —
just watching her rest.

The Things She Does

She leaves cabinet doors open,
every one of them,
like she meant to come back
but never did.
The cap off the toothpaste
so, it hardens overnight.
She steals the blanket
without noticing,
rolled tight in it
while I'm left holding the edge.
She forgets her keys
often,
asks me if I've seen them,
or assumes she threw them away,
checks the counter,
checks upstairs,
checks the counter again.
None of it matters,
not really—
just the small things
you only notice
when you're close enough
to live inside someone's habits.
And the truth is,
I'd miss all of it
if the house ever went quiet.

You're Always There

When I need you most,
you're always there for me.

No matter how I'm feeling
or what mood I'm in,
you shift with me, note for note.

Whether I'm far from home
or lying in my own bed,
you know how to speak to me,
how to get through to me,
saying exactly what I need to hear.

Somehow you understand
what I can't explain,
and you stay with me
until I find my way back.

V — THE UNIVERSE AND US

Evidence of Life

The blankets and comforter thrown across the
bed,
slippers left wherever they were kicked off,
clothes in piles, a bag of books half-spilled.

Dishes stacked in the sink,
animals—our animals—adding their own smell,
shedding, pissing, shitting,
a mess no matter where we're heading.

Holiday décor swapped every season,
half-placed, half-forgotten without much thought.

The garage overflowing with shoes—
tiny ones, muddy ones,
far more than any family needs.

Our folded clothes don't put themselves away;
drawers packed tight, shelves just as crowded.

Trash and recycling piled to the top,
sometimes twice in a single day.

The bathroom counter covered in stuff,
the hamper erupting with clothes.

Boxes of lotions, baskets of wear,
something in every corner.

The nightstand crowded with cups and things,
small reminders of everyday spills.

Across every room—
Legos, notebooks, half-finished projects,
the subtle evidence of growing kids.

And walking through it all,
I catch myself laughing—

because this chaos, this clutter,
this avalanche of everyday life…

it's ours.

Not mine. Not yours.
Ours.

The shape of a family
built by two tired parents
doing their best.
Finding whatever quiet we can.

So, when we get frustrated by the mess,
I try to remember:

we're not fighting the clutter.
We're learning how to live
inside the life we made together—
all five of us.

Forever Unimpressed

Mom's food?
"It's not terrible."
A telescopic view of the moon?
One glance.
A shrug.
"And now what?"
At sixteen,
everything is someone else's fault—
teachers, siblings, the universe,
me, sometimes.
He carries an attitude like armor,
shrugs like punctuation,
moves through the world
with a practiced unimpressed stare.
Nothing is ever quite enough
to move him,
to pull a spark
from behind those blue eyes.
But every so often,
when he forgets to guard it,
I catch a half-smile—
quick, crooked, unplanned—
and suddenly I'm back
to the days when he was small,
his hand wrapped in mine,
looking up at me
like I controlled the world.
Now he barely looks up at all.
But that smile—
that tiny break in the clouds—
reminds me he's still in there,

the boy who was fascinated
by music, cars, dinosaurs,
life and all its wonders.
His guarded way of seeing things
still makes me laugh every time.
Forever unimpressed—
and somehow,
forever mine.

The Rough Road Behind Us

It started off smooth, like a sunny paved
highway—
so new, so easy to trek.
Nothing could get in our way,
both naïve, not knowing what to expect.

Over time we felt the bumps
of an old, worn track.
Life's choices weren't so clear-cut;
we forged ahead without looking back.

The bumps turned into potholes
on a dirt road in the rain.
We dodged them when we could,
but still discovered pain—

But now the rough road is behind us,
and the weather ahead seems clear.
This journey has been treacherous,
yet, I'm proud to call you Dear.

I'm grateful for where we are,
although tattered and bruised.
We've added three beautiful passengers to our
car—
I'd call it more "comfortable" than "used."

We've got a few years on these tires now,
an imbalance of wear and age.
We're soulmates—me for you and you for me—
in this love story, let's turn the page.

No matter the terrain
or the weather in the sky,
the one constant that remains
are always you and I.

The Ride

Riding my bike through a neighborhood
of unfamiliar faces and quiet houses,
my son strapped to the seat behind me,
his small hands resting on my sides
like he trusted the world because he trusted me.
At the end of the street stood a man
I'd already decided not to greet—
old, unfriendly, the kind of face
you avoid because it's easier.
I planned to pass without a word,
pretend we hadn't seen each other.
I was sure he wanted the same.
But before I could turn away,
my son—three years old,
open in a way adults forget—
shouted, "Hi!"
The man's face changed instantly,
like someone had reminded him
he still mattered.
He smiled wide.
He said hello back.
I lifted a hand and waved,
late to the moment.
And just like that,
my boy taught me something
I should have taught him first.
I was proud of him that day.
And quietly ashamed
that he was the one
showing me how to be better.

Thoughts of Home

Days full of stress,
my desk a mess.
The dumb fights,
the long nights—
none of it depends on the address.

Because when I'm with you,
baby, I'm home.

Plans change,
I should go with the flow.
I shouldn't care—
and deep down, I know.

Though the news is bad
and the traffic worse,
all feels right in the world
because, baby, I'm home.

If the weather is wet or dry,
if we're just barely getting by,
it doesn't matter—
baby, I'm home.

When it's tough to weather the storm,
I think of better times
when I was safe and warm.
I can't see the future
beyond the trees,
but with you,
life's a breeze.

Baby, I'm home.

Sometimes it's hard to see—
forgive me, please—
but I'm the happiest I'll be
when I'm home.

And when that sad day comes,
when the kids are grown,
you and I will live the rest of our lives
in the comfort of home.

And long after I'm gone,
when your time finally comes,
I'll be waiting—
right where I've always been—

for you to come home.

Companion

He greets her in the morning with a stretch and a wag,
His tail drumming out a hopeful beat.
She takes him out into the morning air,
Then he runs back in for a treat.
He knows the rhythm of her steps,
Each foot on the floor.
A quiet guard with human eyes,
Who always wants one moment more.
And when she's gone, he takes a rest,
Dreaming of her until the moment she returns.
Whether it's from a long day's work,
Or just a short slip out the door, he yearns.
He patiently waits a lifetime,
Then showers her with joy.
Sometimes she's empty-handed,
And others she'll bring a toy.
He nudges for a walk,
Maybe a trip to the park.
Happy to stay by her side,
From daylight into dark.
And when the night grows still,
He settles without a word.
Nestled against her legs,
A comfort felt, not heard.

Thinking of the Past

I get sad sometimes,
thinking about the way things used to be.
It's hard to stay in the moment
when my mind keeps drifting back.

I remember when you were so tiny—
it feels like yesterday,
and somehow a lifetime ago.

The pinky promises,
the small hands in mine,
the mornings when your smile
made the whole world feel simple.

Even now,
every time I see your face,
that little grin you still share,
I'm reminded that everything
will be alright.

Held to the Light

I remember that day clearly—
her perfume in the air,
flowers opening after rain,
the cool morning before the heat settled in.
The jokes that made us laugh,
the small thing I did that annoyed her,
the kids restless, shifting out of place,
birds chirping, insects buzzing,
the soft click of the camera.
I had no interest in going,
but it became a good day.

Now I see pictures of us from ten years ago.
I don't remember taking them,
or where we were,
or why we were laughing
in that direction.
I don't recognize the people
standing just outside the frame.

One day our children's children
may hold a photo from that morning.
They might ask,
"Is that you as a kid
with grandma and grandpa?
Where were you going?"

Decades later,
the picture may surface again—
pulled from a dusty box,
held up to the light for a moment,

no real thought of who we were
or what the day meant.

Then it will be set aside,
slipped back into the dark,
little evidence left
that we ever existed.

APPENDIX

(Brief notes on selected poems)

I. The World as I See It

III. The Long Look Inward

IV. The Center of Gravity

www.ingramcontent.com/pod-product-compliance
Lightning Source LLC
La Vergne TN
LVHW090536110826
845146LV00003B/1132

* 9 7 9 8 9 9 5 2 1 5 0 1 1 *